Mame, Sol, and Dog Bark

Mame, Sol, and Dog Bark

lynne potts

The National Poetry Review Press
Warrenton, Oregon

The National Poetry Review Press
(an imprint of DHP)
Post Office Box 670, Warrenton, Oregon 97146

Mame, Sol, and Dog Bark
Copyright © 2017 Lynne Potts
All rights reserved

Printed in the United States of America
Published in 2017 by The National Poetry Review Press

ISBN 978-1-935716-41-9

Cover art under license from Shutterstock.com

CONTENTS

SAN FRANCISCO

DAY BEGUN

OUT AND ABOUT WHAT

SAN FRANCISCO

DAY BEGUN

CODIFIED COFFEE

Worn down and fissured park boulders

cling to fog while the city comes slow

to its face, long sleeves of sound:

curb rub and dripped awnings, rill of water

making its way down a cornered window

to street grates, manholes with iron descents

to deep rooms of rubbered cable coil and twist,

the codified connections under a city

bloomed to morning with the phone ringing,

coffee machine gurgling, toast bounced

to another day of beauty and destruction.

PARKING DOWN THE MIDDLE

We'll split it, Sol said, tabled melon waiting
with cleaver

like a Flemish print waiting to be hung
in the hall

like someone sad in a bus station listening
for departures.

Too much talk about what is whose, Mame said.

Can you split a kitchen in half?

Sol was thinking of the past:

trips across the country,

ambling into some atrophied gas station

with Saran-wrapped ham sandwich

his private scenery, a picture he called

Desolation with Promise;

then a two-lane highway with giant neon cactus

in the background, beckoning bus station beyond—

someone he would meet later called Mame.

CURBED AS INTRANSITIVE VERB

Tumble-weeded fog rolled over Mame,

left toe painted red

uncovered at the end of the bed.

Sol left impressions

like an eddy that won't budge

even in great waves or riptides of their lives.

She'd stay put in bed, abide the noise

as a backhoe chewed the street,

spat pebbles to a bucket loader below.

Some days you had to grit your teeth

to get up, she said

for no reason.

AS AIR GOES TO A BALLOON

Hilly city: how does one keep track

of trolley-shuttle ups and downs

when doubt catches the avenue eucalyptus

like a birthday balloon slowly losing air?

Could the sea with its kind of seasoning

be an answer? To what question?

One labored day gives way to another.

Finger the string hanging in the balloon tree

and choose the same route;

as always it leads round and round,

one breath and then another

of questionable texture,

the sequence like string tree-tied

to a postponed present.

IN A SLOUGH OF SLEEP

Sol, suspended, seemed to hang

like a bright-blue kite caught in a cypress

he couldn't climb

even with shoes he'd left in the cellar

where someone stored paint or was it comics

with mildewed covers—

his sleep shifting with steam-kettle sound

coming from across the hazy bay

without requirements or conditions,

which was a relief.

TAXI

It's the world sway, Mame thought and took it back

the word *world*—too grand.

Stand in one place and let the sepia

seep through the drapes was how to see it:

listen to traffic below on its roll to work,

purse with CDs, crackered liverwurst;

taxi zippered with missing teeth

idled at the crossing's bloodshot eyes.

She would be alone with the day's papery news,

sun with its lids down, lowered blinds.

Getting up would come later—when *lethargy*

had passed and she could face the wiry elevator,

its chattering doors, slam-dunk confidence.

NOTHING EVER DRIES IN SAN FRANCISCO

Live in the past, I do, Mame said, slurring words

as an outside crash brought an outburst from Dog Bark,

clatter of cars, crimping fenders folded,

bent rear views.

The brief noise splintered the morning

to slivers Mame couldn't piece

like a puzzle with several missing

as she hung a wet dishcloth on a hook,

waited for a dash of sun.

Once she was almost happy in Spain

which had an abundance of sun,

but she'd learned; she wouldn't look back in

memory's glass she knew to be convex,

inclined to distortion.

ROLLING A CITY TO WORK

Fog rolls the city to a ball hid behind a hill,

nob of *disappear*—then gutter-grate toes,

ankle curbs, streetlight shins rising like

palimpsests of yesterday,

the day before, the day before that

each pasted in a scrapbook

pages turned brown

some things loosed and slipping out—

the city itself slipping into something else,

not laced or silk, something more prosaic:

pin-stripe, perhaps, on a serge for work.

Wander off was Mame's habit, antidote

to periodic obsessions.

Today she would go to the aquarium

where, in a delirium of fish, she'd lose track of time.

Take the carp at the bottom of the tank:

thank God she couldn't see what they ate

gulp by swiveled gulp, diver a-goggle, bilging sharks.

It's *domestic distance* that causes swillings

along the bottom, she thought

later, pulling ribbons from roses

she had just bought—

its ends, a serrated mess.

HEXED

A textbook case of mental parvenu never more

than opaque; scratch on isinglass so viewers

would misconstrue meaning.

In the mirror she held a face of discontent

facing distortions of all kinds—

hummers and hand grenades and angry

jaws set like plaster of Paris masks.

Once she had wanted so much;

now all she wanted was to search alleys

with her mind like a sieve, hoping to catch

little objects only: bottle of cardamom,

shoe tree with a broken heel, twisted stainless whisk.

NO SHOWMANSHIP

Mame stayed home. Again.

Trapped in a hairnet of thought

that wouldn't untangle even when a blimp

floated by a living room window,

hovered over Alcatraz

and slid on by.

What's goes on in the mind of a prisoner

she wondered, flocculating the chenille,

balling it to throw at Bark. *How to escape?*

The mind would always do that.

Couldn't it, for once, just sit still in a body,

forget the jot or tittle,

tangles of what would always be a puzzle.

Then she put her head down and cried—

for the prisoners, of course.

ALCATRAZ

Ominous, bizarre sound *alc* holding the tongue down

to close the throat, hiss of *az* as it slips a snake from
your lips,

arch authority of stiff-back *A*, swastika of the final *z*.

There it sits, rock with iron bars, chains

to keep evil from slipping over edges
into the Bay—

its flowery aqua gown, flush-pink city so innocent.

Try as you may to ignore it (make a country or love
perfect)

each time you turn the corner of the street

or come down the crook of Lombard,
staff of Van Ness

you see bars and braces trying to make

your mind be straight.

While I'm gone, hollow of words Mame knew

would swallow her in ominous-ness.

Open the reprieve purse of *while* and you see

coins spill through a tear in the bottom.

While was everywhere: someone waiting for her
to find keys,

a car by the side of the road in a thunderstorm,

where you take your clothes off feverishly—

space between now and death that has to be filled

though always empties just as quickly.

OUT AND ABOUT WHAT

BRIDGE, PAGODA, PURSES

Three Chinese fishermen,

poles in hand, cross a porcelain

plate in the De Young Museum:

stream under the bridge,

settled boulders,

ancient blue boats at the shore.

Women behind the pagoda,

kneaded sheep and ox hides,

dry stomach, hoof, butchered side.

In San Francisco, women

carry leather purses

with faux gold latches

to their offices on Market.

Out the office windows: bridges

over the China-blue Pacific.

LET'S GO TO THE DESERT

Is that what she said?

Another trek to *Nowhere* was what Sol thought:

desert, a labyrinth without hedges,

mazes of aridity

even Ezekiel couldn't tolerate—

heat poured past thermometer's lip,

scorched throat.

From where in Mame's soul came such a wish?

A dish of sand with no rim, heat-glazed platter

of prickles for those with no taste!

Ezekiel's place of wander-dust, not Sol's.

Can't you just stay put, her mother used to say

when she was sick with a fever.

Now it wasn't what she wanted.

SORTING THE PANTRY BEFOREHAND

*A sardine's a sad thing, especially the tinned type
for a picnic,* Sol said.

They had agreed on Diamond Heights Park
with Dog Bark, of course.

Mame, lost in thought, put down a basket of
bread and cheeses,

spread the ground for a table.

Sardines see all, she said, staring at tinfoil eyes
in their oily bed.

What did it matter what happened later when
she caught

the table cloth on a crusted wrought-iron fence;

unraveled was a calmer state of mind.

She'd been that way since before Sol knew when.

SUICIDE, A GOLDEN GATE

Golden Gate Bridge drops coins to bay

waters below waves carrying them to sea

until dumped in some secret place only

fake rainbows know.

Some have thought to dive

for them but no one's ever

made it past the chimera of what they

thought could be had

or escaped.

A zippity do-dah day for Mame

who had too few since August when depression
clotted like milk.

Awful was what Sol said; glad it was over—

then to her and Dog Bark *Let's go to Marin.*

Frilled in a fuchsia boa and baseball cap
(Mame in both)

they rode the bridge in sun the color

of chrome on old Chrysler bumpers.

For lunch: cucumber on pumpernickel

hardly worth the paper tablecloth it was served on

but worth all whiles of being together:
shared afternoon

of amplitude as in *You are my sunshine...*

Yes, they had ordered a Zip Car
for the excursion

to live on the lam, Sol called it
a *Hey-Why-Not* day.

EXTRA COAT

Mame preferred fur on the collar only

russet brown and not too new;

an indulgence as was Dog Bark

padding carpets with his sallow smile

his need for her pleasing them both

as she poured kibbles to an orange dish,

cats running the border in a spree
of tiger-ness.

She collared Bark, brushed his coat,

took him for a walk to pick rose hips
and honeysuckle

for a boat-shaped vase, as she said

to herself: *Wouldn't it be nice to sail*
(in alpaca, of course)

to the Antarctic or maybe the tropics

decked out in linen and voile for dinner.

Then thinking of Sol's ambient humor

and Bark wagging the kitchen for lunch

she rescinded wishing.

CAUGHT BETWEEN REDEMPTION
AND A SANDCASTLE

Knur-knuckled old woman easing
a grocery cart

down the curb over a rattled gutter bottle where
a Chinese man

organizes a bewildered collection for
CVS redemption,

music shop metronome wagging its
tick-tocky finger;

face of the clock, Fourth Street Station,
a hundred hands waving the scene

turning to water

Fort Point or Baker Beach where a pair
of hands make a funnel

to sift warm sand onto a woman's breast,
knee joint,

hands digging a moat by a castle with stick flag.

Then the scene back to the city, adroit window
washer

with squeegee on the 70th floor etched blue

in the plate glass as someone turns to catch

him falling asleep as in a dream she awakens.

MEET ME AT THE MOVIES

If life could be drawn as a pie chart,

how big a slice was his job, Sol wondered,

working numbers to ensure safe risks:

actuary, which didn't actually define him—

more calculator, keenly distracted.

Clearly the mind constantly surfs

the indeterminate, he said to himself;

to Mame, *Did you see "Children of Paradise?"*

Now there's a job: miming!

Gestures so you don't have to talk,

the world a skip and a hop with

only yourself to hear what you're saying.

LOMBARD STREET

Cobbled sounds of city granite loud
and oyster soft

familiar as old sun porch curtains or a bicycle

coming down the block with empty basket,
horn stuck.

Coddled too like certain moods—say between
ordering a pastrami sandwich

and staying on top of the blankets when your
shoes are wet from puddles in the Castro

coddle also the tepid way you descend Lombard five
miles an hour as the city soars above—

flowers and cobbles with it you think,
though the street's been there

more than two centuries. Trust it.

WHAT IS THE RUSH?

Poppies were pink-to-red orange

thin necks, cushy palms

climbing the cerulean blue

so Sol stopped the car for a view.

Wholly solid, he thought:

the bolder coast of California,

breccia showing the way

Earth began, coming from below,

waves washing bones to limey green

laying them, lazy, on the packed sand.

Then picking a handful of poppies

to look closer at their seedy centers,

wondering how long they would last,

thin stems on a watch turning the hours.

SAN FRANCISCO:
DOWN BY THE BUENA VISTA

Fishing skiffs bump along the docks,

ropes and cords slap the water

making reckless curls and ringlets

down the neck of the harbor;

water beyond, white,

capped and unruly:

wayward like giggling girls in Puritan pews

destabilized by sex, buoyed and bobbing:

frizzle-headed lunatics who would be caught,

of course, taught a lesson for laughing—

those scowly men out to catch girls

in their Biblical nets.

MIST IN LEVITATE

Mist lifted by hill-hung pulleys,

curtains in levitate of wait and anon,

cumulus brew as another appears.

On and on, chambers of haze in rise
and disappear,

rent seams and backward-shadow caught:

fog aggrieved and occluded
fingering a coat hem

remembering good-by waves
to smudged train windows.

DECLINING DAY

Stalking her heart, its runaway cattails,

marsh-grown grasses dried to sludge,

backlash, flotsam,

Sol tried to be patient—slushing away

in the unknown, misbegotten

slipstreams of affection.

Here's what he put together:

his fiery feelings for Mame,

or a vacant day in the marshes

with fishing rod and sandwich.

He listened to his heart,

its incursions, dark disturbances;

when he got home found a melon

she had bought; sliced it, ate the better half.

SOFA

The flip side of Mame's lethargy

was hysterical maneuvering

of furniture and knick-knacks

nicked when they were moved,

lightweight behavior she knew to be

a foibled course of action.

It's what happened every time a new set

of gods died:

Ra, Baal, Jehovah, Zeus, philosophers too.

More recently: cosmic incidents.

So reality preyed—and that was that.

She thought the sofa should go

after the piano, to hide the table legs.

It was comic relief, also redundant.

Take how fire swept Chinatown:

Some said, *Good. Now it's clean,*

but tongues say one thing and worse—

licking to bedrooms, chewed paper walls,

black lungs snaking kitchens to swallow

spoons, kettles, slippers under the table.

Who screams through the corridors

in a dragon city swinging tail fire all

directions?

Oh, it was not just the Chinese poor.

Fire ate thousands—

many aged who couldn't run

ahead of the licking—

bone ash in mop pails for years.

THE CRUX

In the wistfulness of her unsure,

blousy moods, dour drifting

to chocolate shops, drugstore

pepper/salt shakers

papier-mâché toucans with viridian eyes,

Mame spotted a bouquet of haulm,

switchy and unkempt in a dusty dentist office

which spun her mind to meridians—

a high-hallelujah sun spiking the day,

pitching it on to a sliding parabola,

in afternoon shadow.

Back home Dog Bark hit the counter

for a bowl of whatever.

Yes, it was slipping to the witching hour

when her mind felt stitched to a gauzy

memory,

haunts of what happened, forbidden,

when she'd needed something spiked

all right

as with a couple of olives.

WELL, THERE'S A PRETTY PARTY

Like the dull lemon scent in egg-drop soup,

plans for a party were a lost

cause not *to be* explained.

Whiskey and patent leather were a given

proof that a party could happen

but risky, as they both knew.

Knew what?

No. Pray for a slatch between waves

(crime or some horrid tidal washing the city).

Give a bash, Sol said, the mixer (a lemon)

but good for Bloody Marys: Tabasco,

horseradish, Worcestershire

in a V-8 engine!

Let's do it, Mame said, though she was soon

drinked out:

a washed-up bottle, she said, looking for a

message.

HANGMAN? YOU GO FIRST

Everyone loves a circus tense with lavender,

yellow, black beaded cords

tied to the Earth, wind in bunting above.

Would the trainer lose a leg to the lion

children asked and didn't laugh.

It had happened once and could again.

Cough drops were candy when you were
little;

it was the sugary spittle that counted,

spotlights spinning tight-rope walkers

to the organ's mezzo-soprano.

Would the pink one in the sequins fall?

Would the tiger make it through the hoop of fire?

All the dangers that never happen,

all the ones that do.

FAILED

Take how light gets bottled up, splintered
into color

in such a fashionable way: sequence of sequins

right after the footlights come up.

She was beautiful.

But it didn't last long, the acting out

of herself: *mannequin of mannerisms*

she had said and dropped it for painting.

Part-time.

How do you part time was what

dogged her during evening's sixes and sevens

lilies closing petals—part herself, part not.

Take Vermeer. Look and look

'til you see through to what

he did you couldn't do.

ASSORTED PREPOSITIONS

High, yes, a heinous habit

of the postmodern mind,

Mame's more lathered than usual.

She called it a *stop* to the mundane:

a time *druthered* than now.

Hadn't people always wanted that?

It was Dog Bark who broke the prattle.

She'd told him "Stop" and he couldn't.

Sol knew it, but he let her be

what she'd become:

alternating affection and affliction.

Who hadn't been, he asked, one way or
another,

in/over/under/addled by one addiction or another?

ENDURANCE AS BOLLARDS

Cast the boat's line in a day's groggy mizzen

ventilated by a throttle-powered, hand-held motor

un-muffled, bottled, about to break up the Bay,

cloud cover like a gavel held up to drop on the table

crazed (as Stubbs would say of Ahab wailing

deck-bound for a nose-less phantom),

day's mist a rag soaked in cleaning-lady

sorrow so deep only the Pacific could cover its
churned flues, subconscious obsessions,

bogged freighters lugging their way to piers,

bollards part in water and under cover of fizzling fog

which is how a city suffers itself, enduring,

vulnerable as blubber, halved and eventually
quartered.

TOOLING THE KITCHEN

Plumb the idea of *attach* meant as soul-to-object;

for example: Mame kept:

*   a pill box of baby teeth

*   pressed buffalo nickels in cardboard

*   stamps with miniscule flags

of Iceland, Bulgaria, Sri Lanka.

It was a hang-on instinct Sol saw as fear

of being two-timed: left and bereft.

I will never never leave, Mame said,

but she meant herself.

AFTER SOL'S TRIP TO THE OUTBACK

Drop shrimp from the list, he said

to the vendor at the counter

in front with fish of marble-green eyes,

darning-needle teeth

fins of tissue and straight pins.

How many millennia between a platypus and this?

Sol asked before dinner

pointing to the oysters with their

slippery eyes, double chins.

This is the last thing I'll ask,

spilling Tabasco in the form

of a question mark on his plate

amused by the coincidence:

co-existence of oyster and himself,

and indeed, the time between.

CHINESE NEW YEAR

Tempest of red crepe and tissue

dragoned its way down Van Ness Ave,

some in drag, pressing their way

to the gyrating eye of the storm.

Year of the Dog, getting its flamboyant start

with the ting, tang, bong of drums

making the Rooster passé; show of gaiety:

foot-long plastic horns effusively blown. *Lords of lantern and super-accelerated laboratory,*

Sol said of the Chinese whom he admired;

Dog was his sign. (Bark's too.)

It was ending for a year he hoped would be better,

but Chinese knew how to call a sign, all right.

Dogs: *loyal and honest, adoring, not caring for wealth.*

Mame, a rooster: *hating to fail, loner behavior.*

Floating city of porcelain pink buildings

cascading streets to pools of musk mallow,

trellises of light through Pacific Heights houses

shops on Geary, blown glass lemon drops,

even Haight Ashbury's funk and panhandle grit,

a glitter beholden to nothing but sky and bridges

which, in their delicate swagger, make no attempt

to contain the flotsam pushing its way patiently,

bumpy but buoyant, out to sea.

ENDINGS

EARTHQUAKES AND A BLIND MAN

Mame had a headache, easy guess

given her medical chart (title to interiors)

decades of obsession which tended to persist:

planet sneaking up, worry of tectonic breaks

and all the little people above.

Balance your plate, Sol said, when their street

stuttered. Maybe it was just the trolley,

Tiresias leaning walls in every city

calling out what it is to be blind.

CITY INSIDE A CITY

Swimming blue light of triumph,

flags flouncing, buntings aloft, light

off puddles with little girls skipping

in sneakers hopping the length of a rope.

But when tragedy comes to a city,

clouds burning, low fog over gutters

turned to ice, one can't know how thick

it will be for breathing or how a girl

in a dirty nightie will cough while

a father calls down the rickety stairwell

to no one coming with towel and kettle

of steaming water for opening her lungs.

BATTLE OF THE NERVOUS

Which of the slurred notes hit by a piano

hammer broke him, Sol had to ask

just back from another apology.

Mame sat on the beach, out of reach

as usual.

Sol struck a B minor, heard a disconnect

through the screen door

which was only a cormorant,

thrown off by the fall of evening.

Minor notes are bone-flat, Sol thought,

even during August reprieves—

breeze off the sea,

war lust in a trough of quiet.

Why did they say *play* the piano?

It was much more difficult.

SORDID THROUGH

The world still had its cherry pits
you could spit

during backyard parties—bit of a gaff,

Dog Bark, his tail caught in the spigot

making everyone laugh.

The water from the garden hose was a rainbow

doing the Lindy Hop. *Very limey*, someone said.

Who fashioned the world so, and so

nothing made sense enough

to get by, Sol thought—

spiraling strings in the ether, gyrating quarks.

Just then Dog Bark flipped around to find his tail

in a thin arc of rainbow—

which was when the party turned rowdy;

as Mame moved the spigot not to hit Bark
but some of the others.

JUST IN FROM THE BACK PORCH

Love, Mame thought, was

a longing that lurked in the rafters

traveling down a spider's thread

to the living room

of a Michigan summer cottage.

Dottle is what's left of a pipe dream

to have that old cottage back.

Then she put a pot in the sink

and remembered the bobber

on the bamboo pole she used

to catch tangerine-bellied sun fish.

It was Delft-day blue out the window

between the swaying bridges.

Love, for Sol, was how a spider seems

suspended without having to hang on

to anything

until threatened

which is when it bites.

ACCIDENT IN THE BREEZY WAY

Schooled as fish in a frenzy-cluster

making anonymous decisions as many or one would,

the city in its flowered apron

painted pearls, Cezanne prints in a shop window

about to close for lack of vision or division.

Sol knew everything made (as quirky Calder
knew too in a wiry way)

comes from tension between two.

So why wonder if a plate is dropped, haddock spilled

since all was not lost?

SEX, POSSESSED, HE

Small of her back was where Sol's love

settled, pooled a deep well-being

as when he found his way interior;

she, a smooth slipped S of a violin,

he, pulling tone from hollows

like a clay urn, lowered

to reach some dark water

deep as the Earth.

Knobbed whelk was beach slush behaving badly

*   like Feverfew that wouldn't take to a
window box

*   like Mame, boxed in by her own talk

(a detached habit of skewed truth).

Addicts in Golden Gate Park did it, too.

It was holiday high season that even

the Buddhists in Marin couldn't resist

(celebration, incantation, packed pillows);

she saw it all as an excuse for libation

(which she would overdo).

It would all be over soon, she said

all just ways to await the end:

a weight, the end.

RYE

Mame knew his body, knew its hollows and spells,

its moon-tides, oracles, the root of him.

If a body meet a body, comin' through the rye,

is there a rush of high wires?

If a body stayed a body all day long

things would work out perfectly,

she'd say to Sol with a wry smile—

body being what it is: permanently temporary.

RUNNING BOARDS NO LONGER EXIST

Love of languor made Mame

linger over a cooling cup of coffee.

Sol waited outside, knotted necktie

hating to be late.

Once, they were running for a trolley

when Mame tripped on the track lattice.

A stranger pulled them aboard.

(*It was a love triangle*, Mame said.)

It made her think of tarsi bones she'd broken

once boarding a freighter.

Sol had wrapped them in gauze.

He kept them together.

SPOOLING HUM

You know night city's hum rounding Market

to Embarcadero through alley throats,

mouthfuls of trash. You hear soft

whistles of wind over Coke bottles,

muffled cough

of a pillowed bundle on a park bench

as the blanket slips to the blacktop.

Who said it's quiet at night? As though

noise could be calibrated, assigned a color—

honking shade of fuchsia or flopped

awning frayed to decayed-tooth blue,

day noise too cacophonous to be caught

by pitch pipe or tuning fork,

night's long, even pitched-thread

unspooling itself around the world

in a D minor mood.

Doodled on the mind's margins

Mame and Sol (Dog Bark too)

waft through San Francisco seasons

and out the window where we see them

waving, waving—unfinished, unrefined, yet

in the jiggered bits and swim of things,

existing—Mame, chewing her thumb,

dance dressed, toe shoed,

Sol shushing Bark with a bone.

As true to life as anything I tell you—

as true as anything.

Acknowledgments

I lived three thousand miles away from San Francisco when I first became obsessed with the city and this fictitious couple. I wish to thank the Virginia Colony for the Creative Arts for providing the time and space to write these poems about them—and to C.J. Sage at the National Poetry Review Press for designing and publishing the book.

Richard Howard, Lucie Brock-Broido, Mary Rueffle, and Mary-Jo Bang were teachers to whom I am forever indebted. I am also grateful to Nance Van Winckel who helped in the editing. Special thanks to poet friends Brian Burt, Kirun Kapur, Mike Perrow, Beth Platow, Kate Westhaver, and Leslie Williams for their continued camaraderie and generous encouragement. And as always, to Gardiner Hartmann.